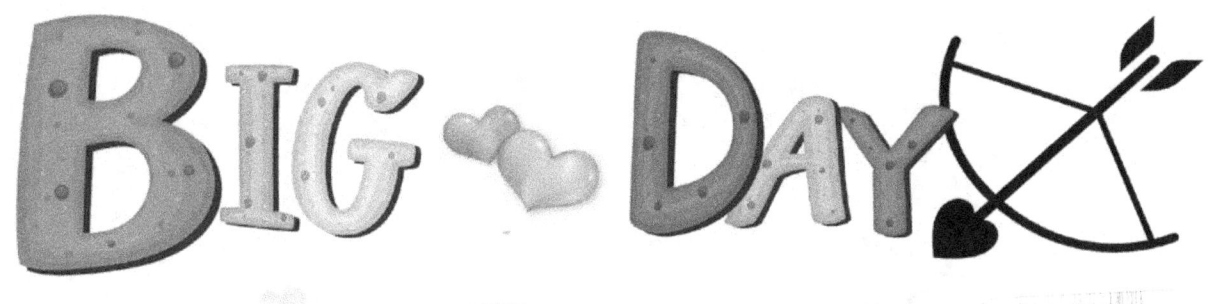

BIG DAY
the wedding
coloring book for kids

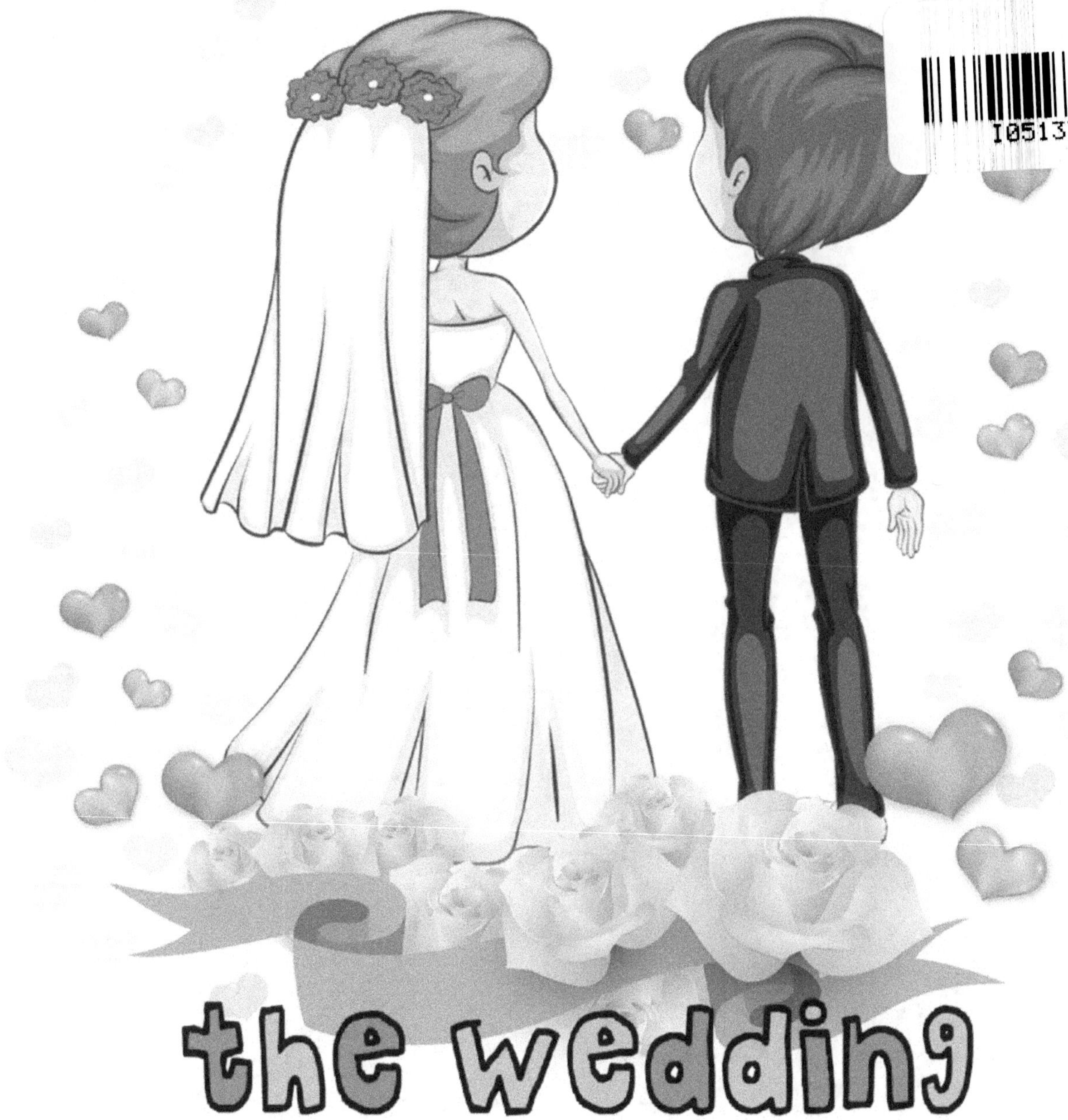

by nina packer

Big Day : The Wedding Coloring Book for kids

Copyright: Published in the United States by Nina Packer

All rights reserved. No part of this publication may be reproduced, stored in retrieval system, copied in any form or by any means, electronic, mechanical, photocopying, recording or otherwise transmitted without written permission from the publisher. Please do not participate in or encourage piracy of this material in any way. You must not circulate this book in any format Nina Packer does not control or direct users' actions and is not responsible for the information or content shared, harm and/or actions of the book readers.

ISBN: 9781720044031

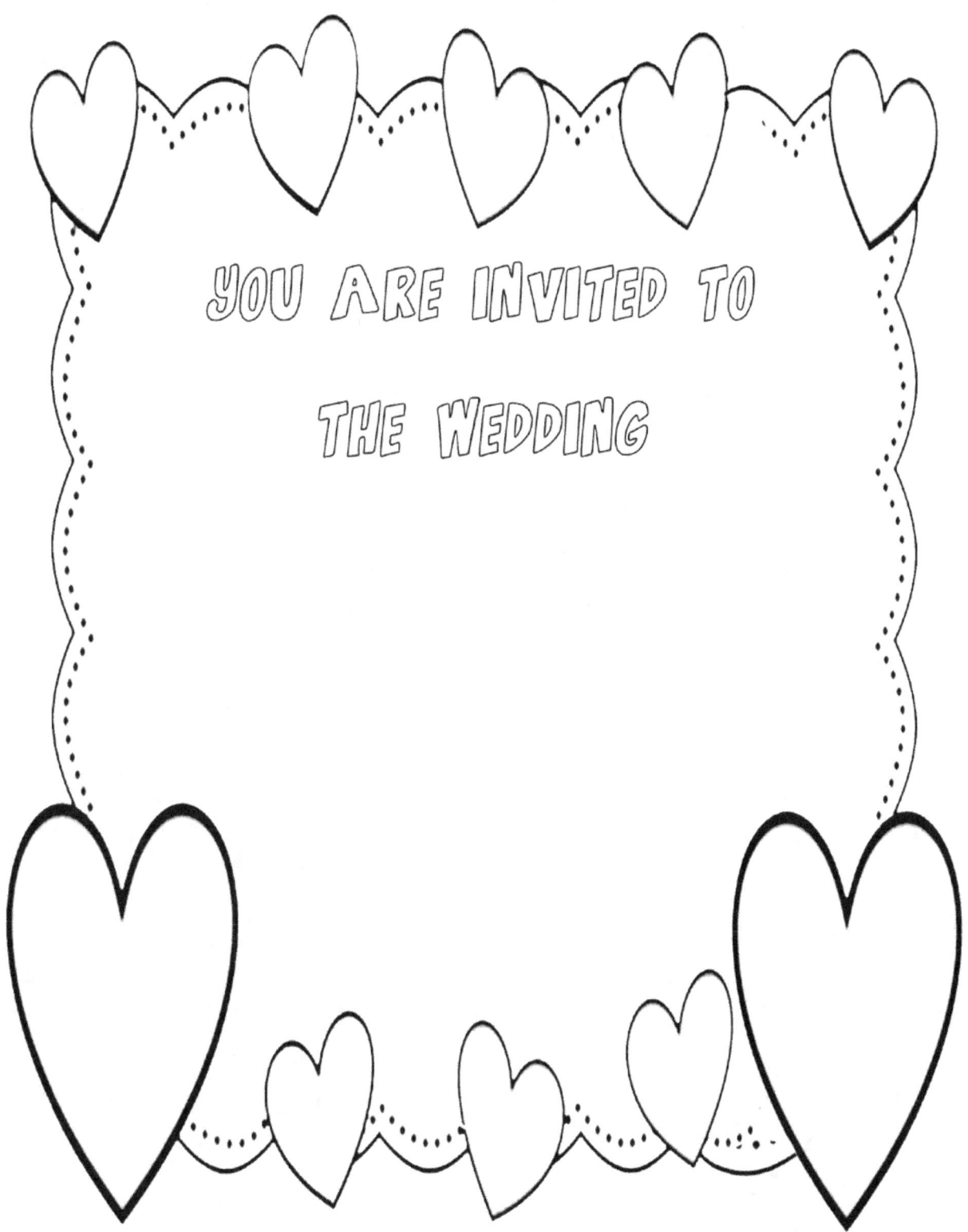

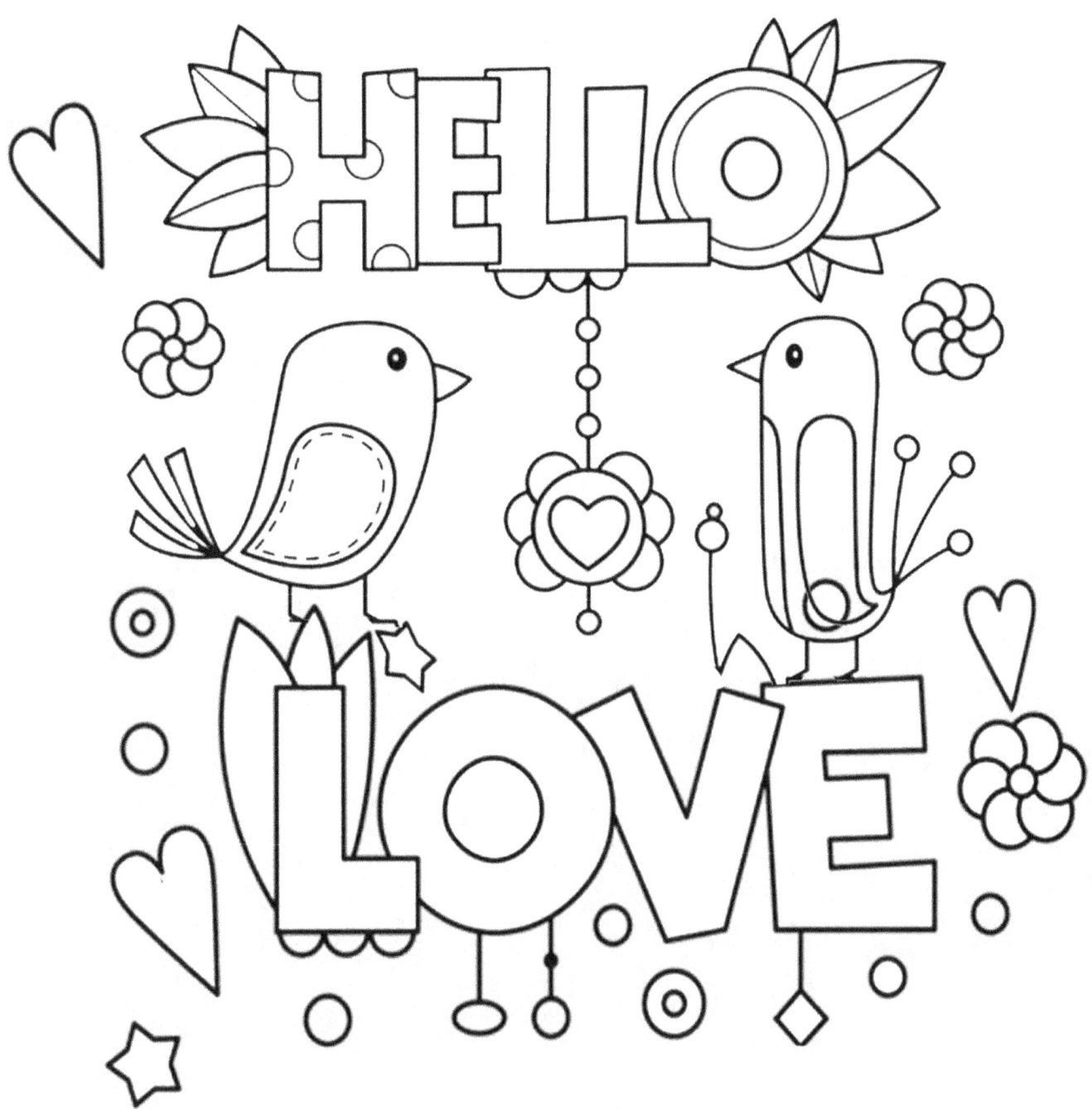

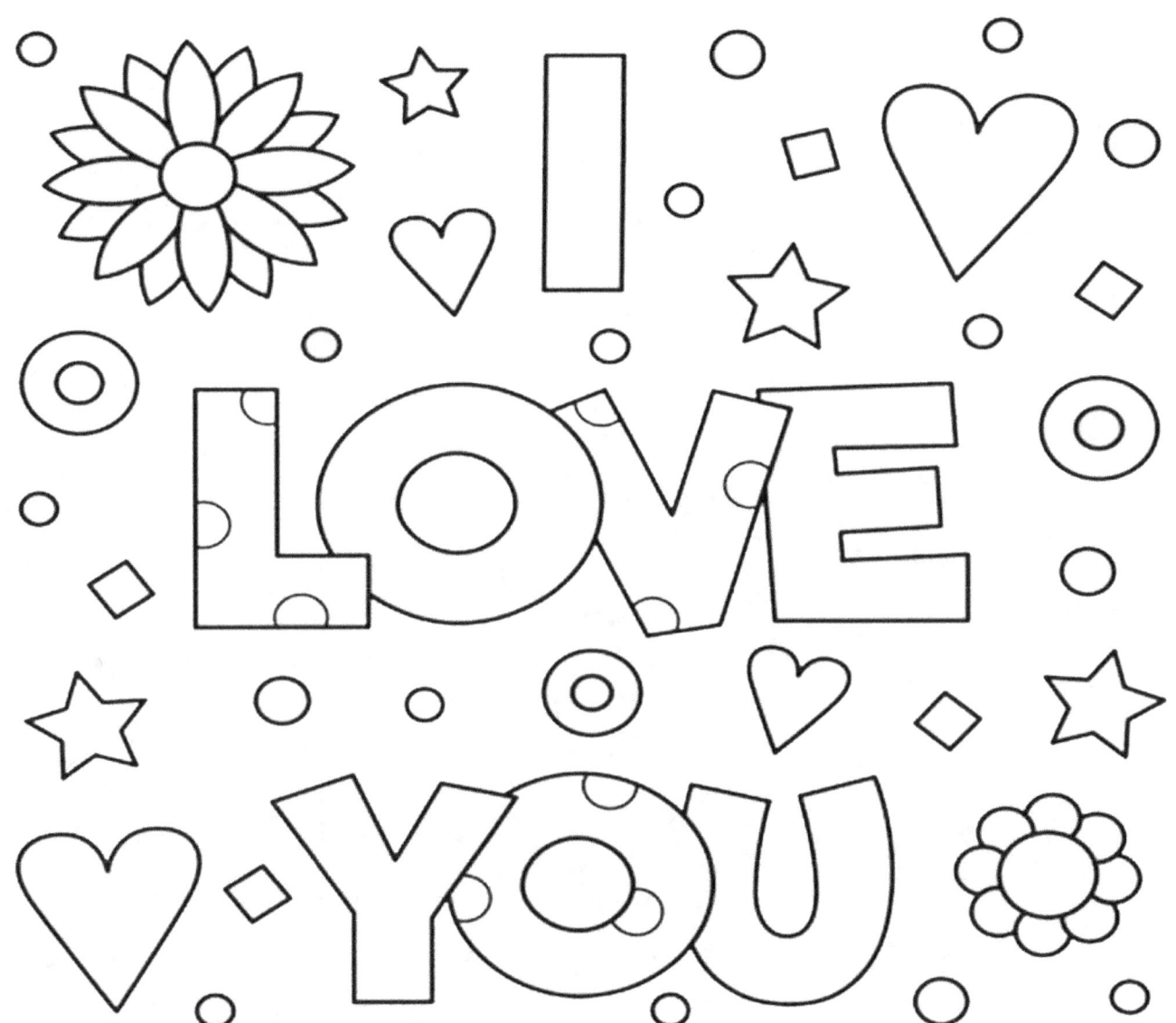

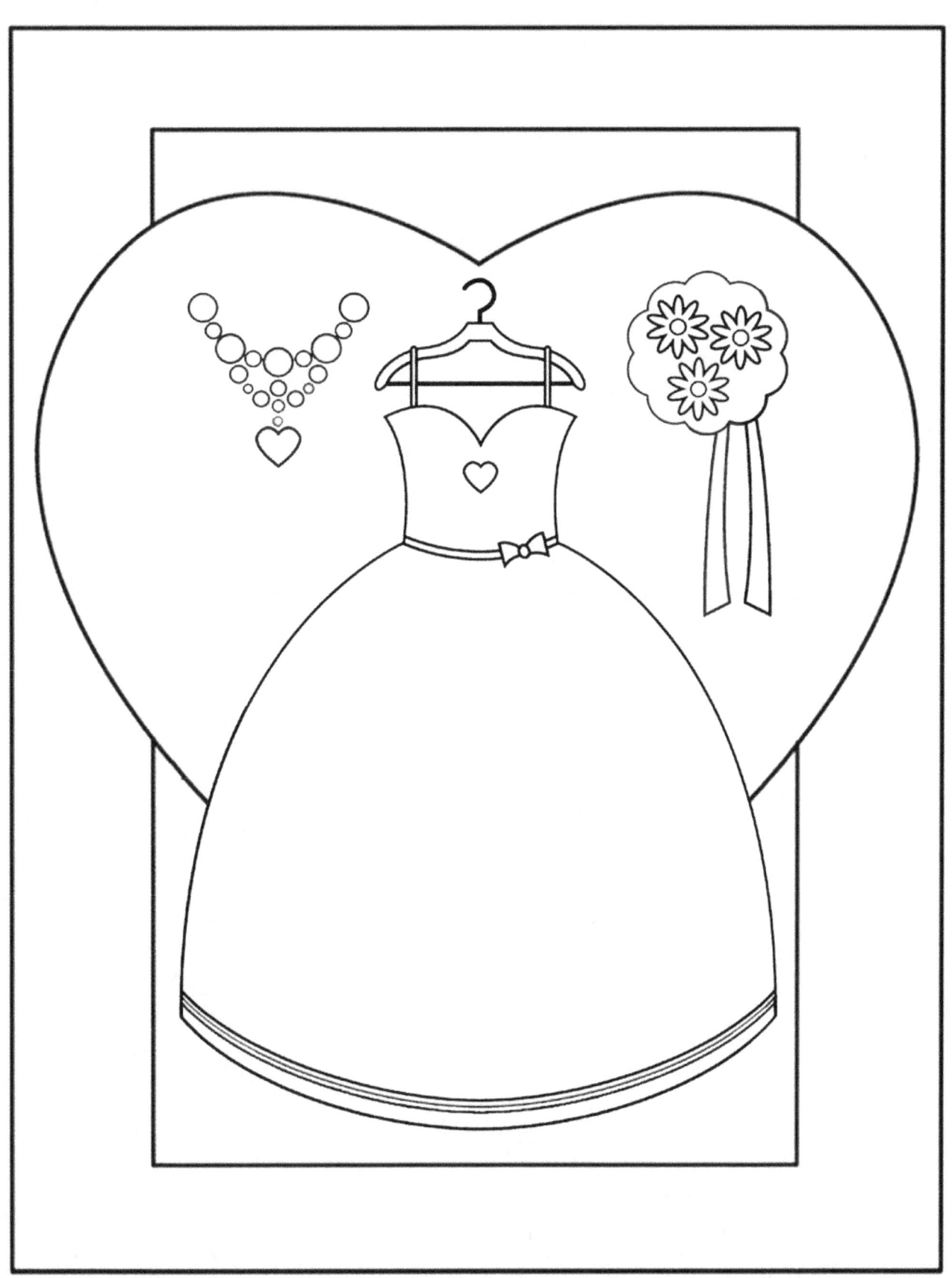

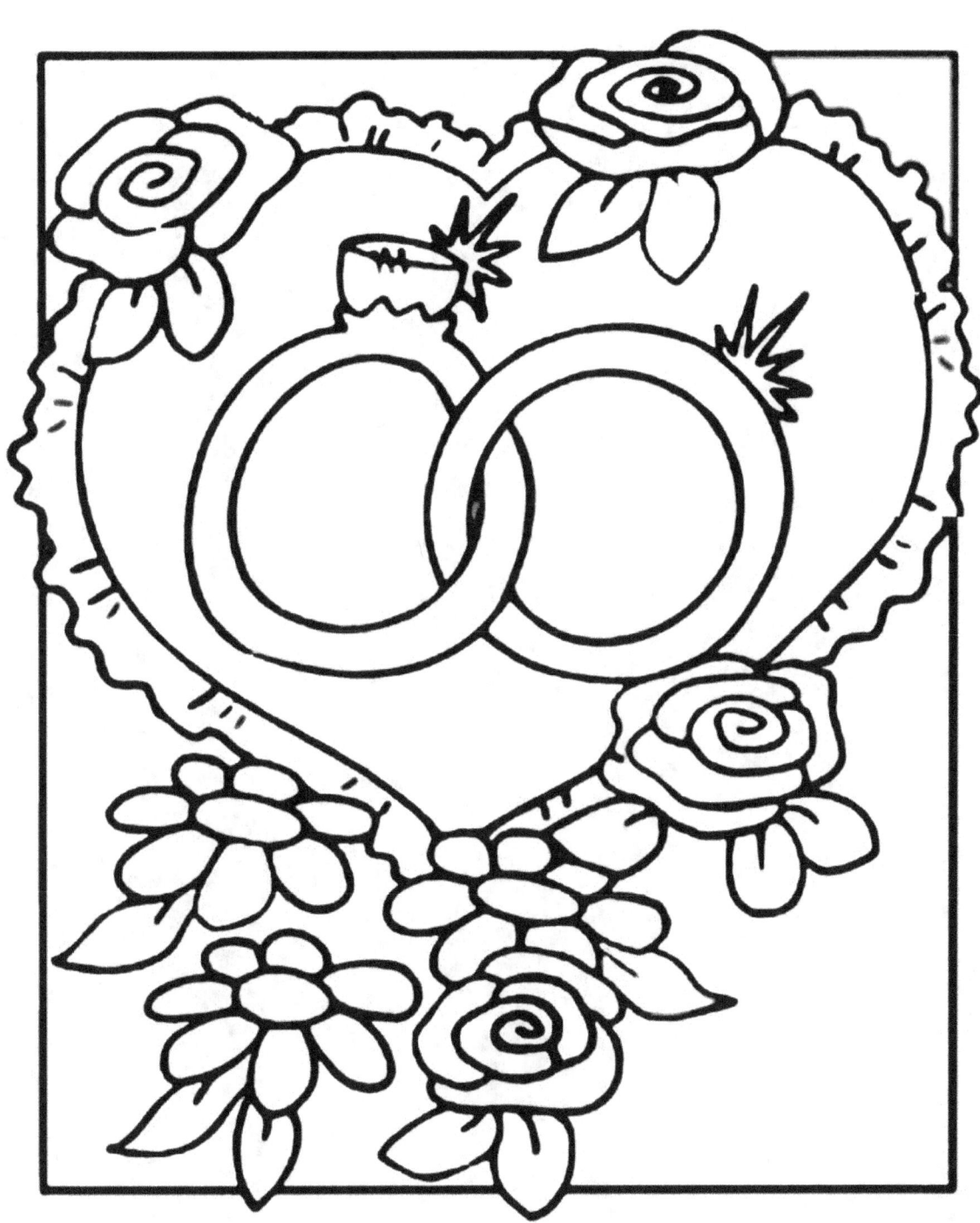

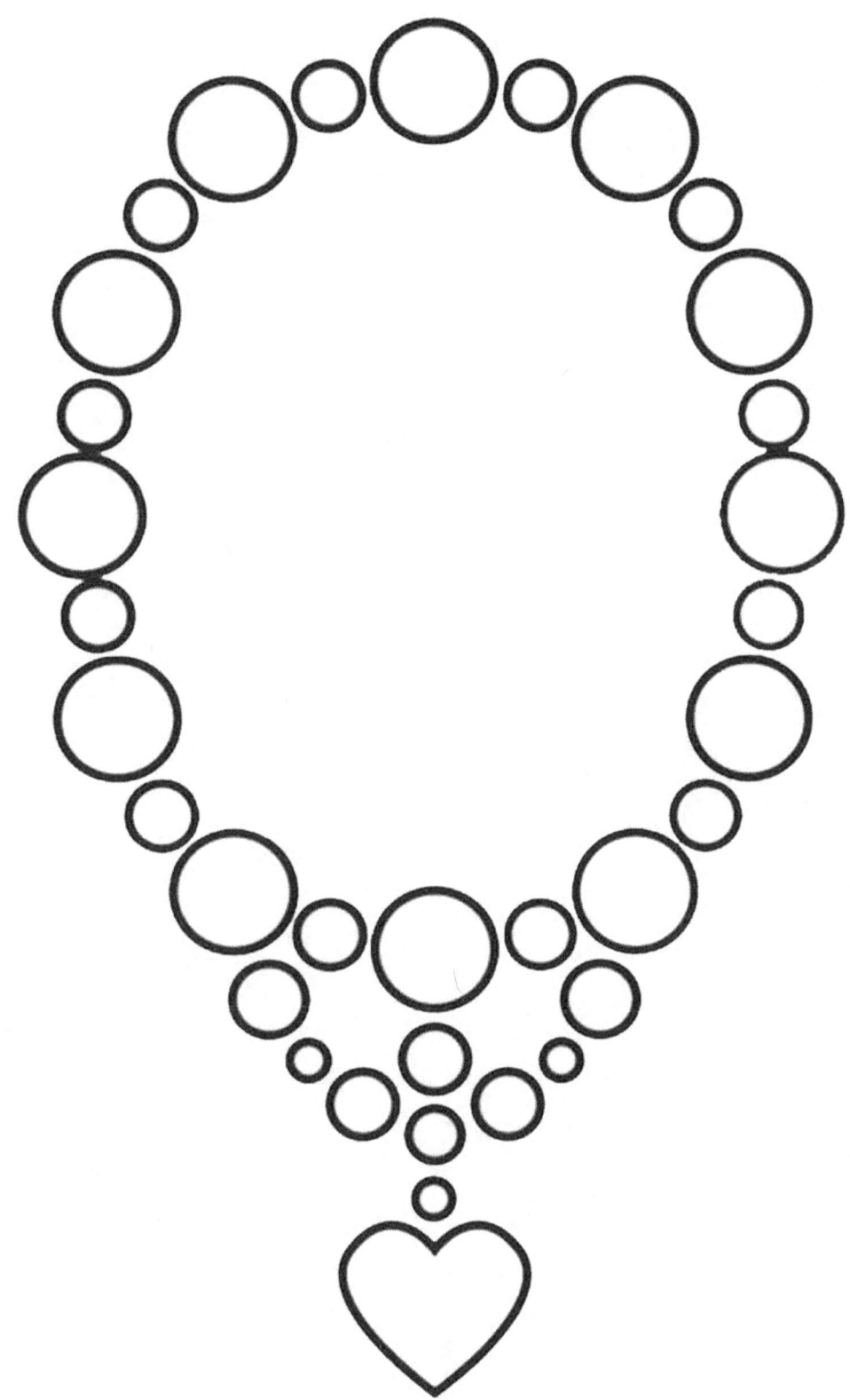

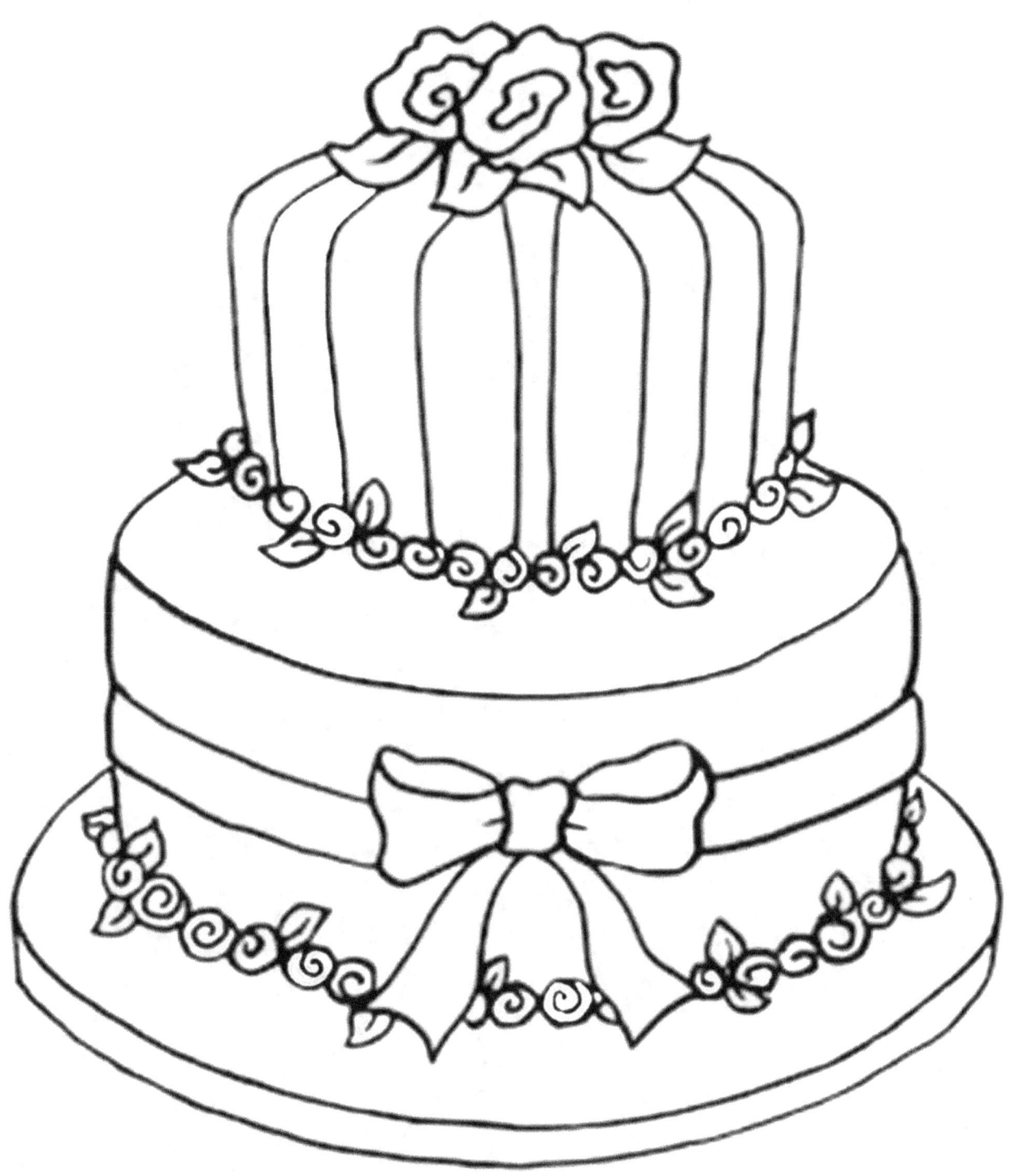

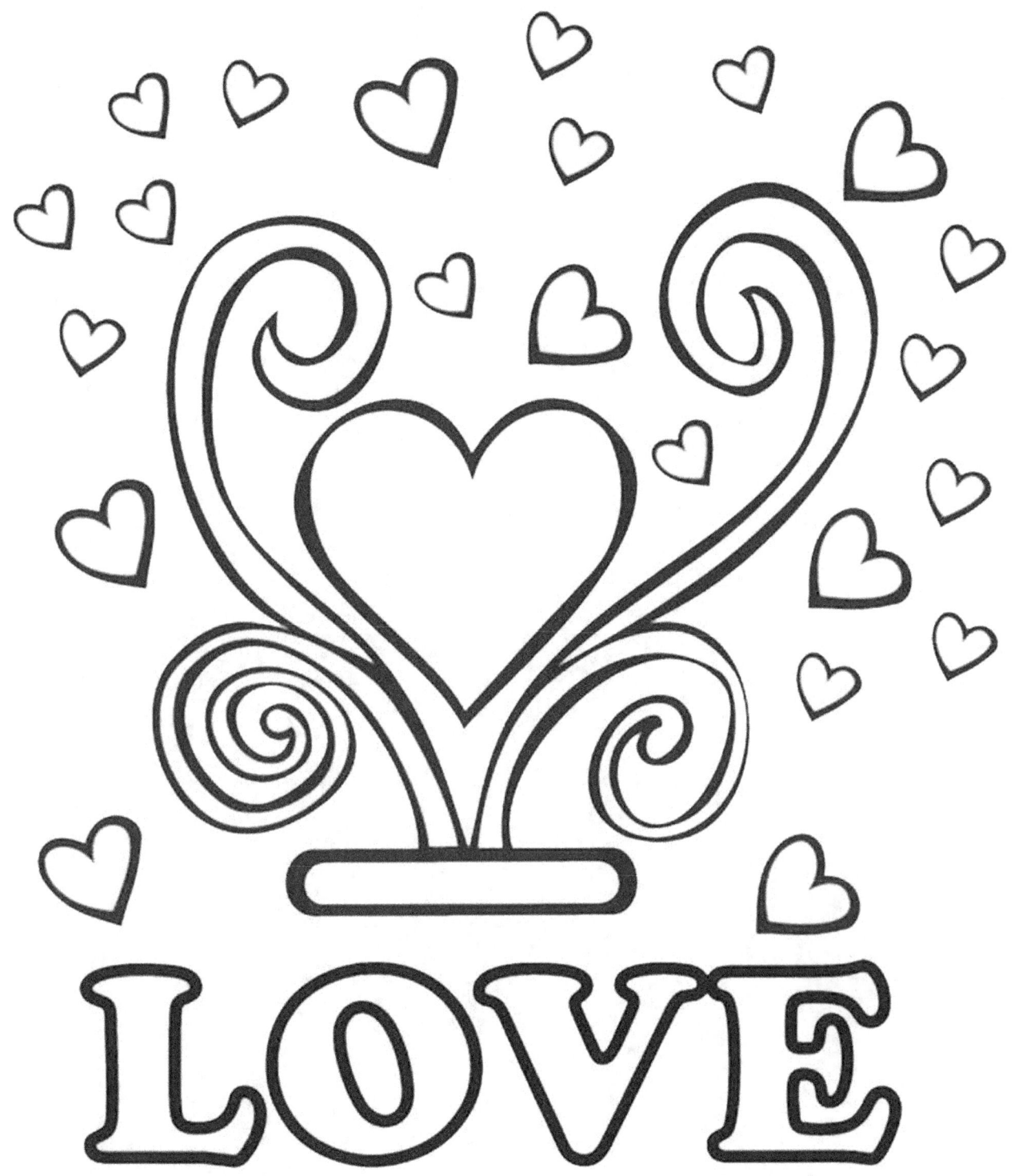

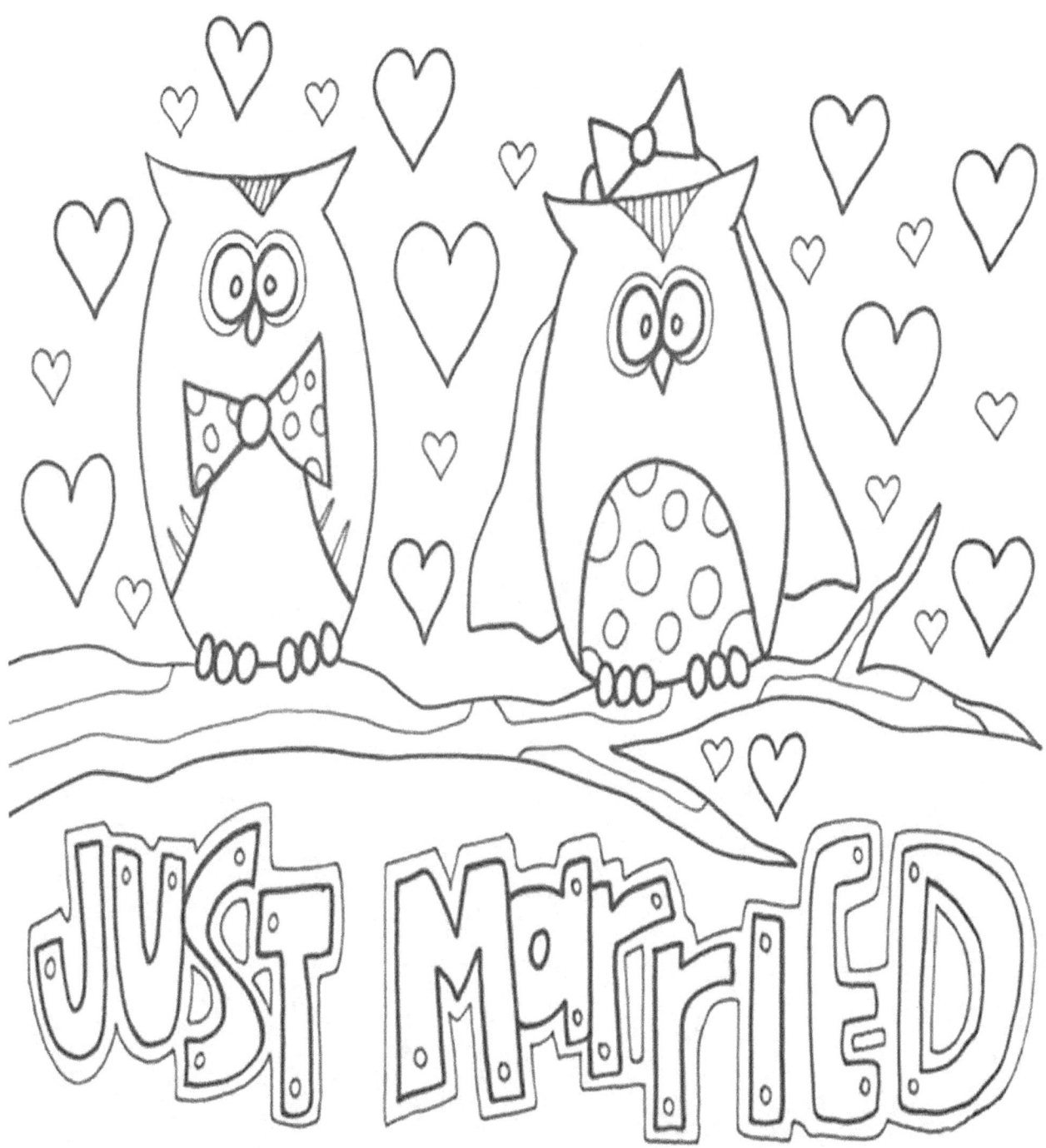

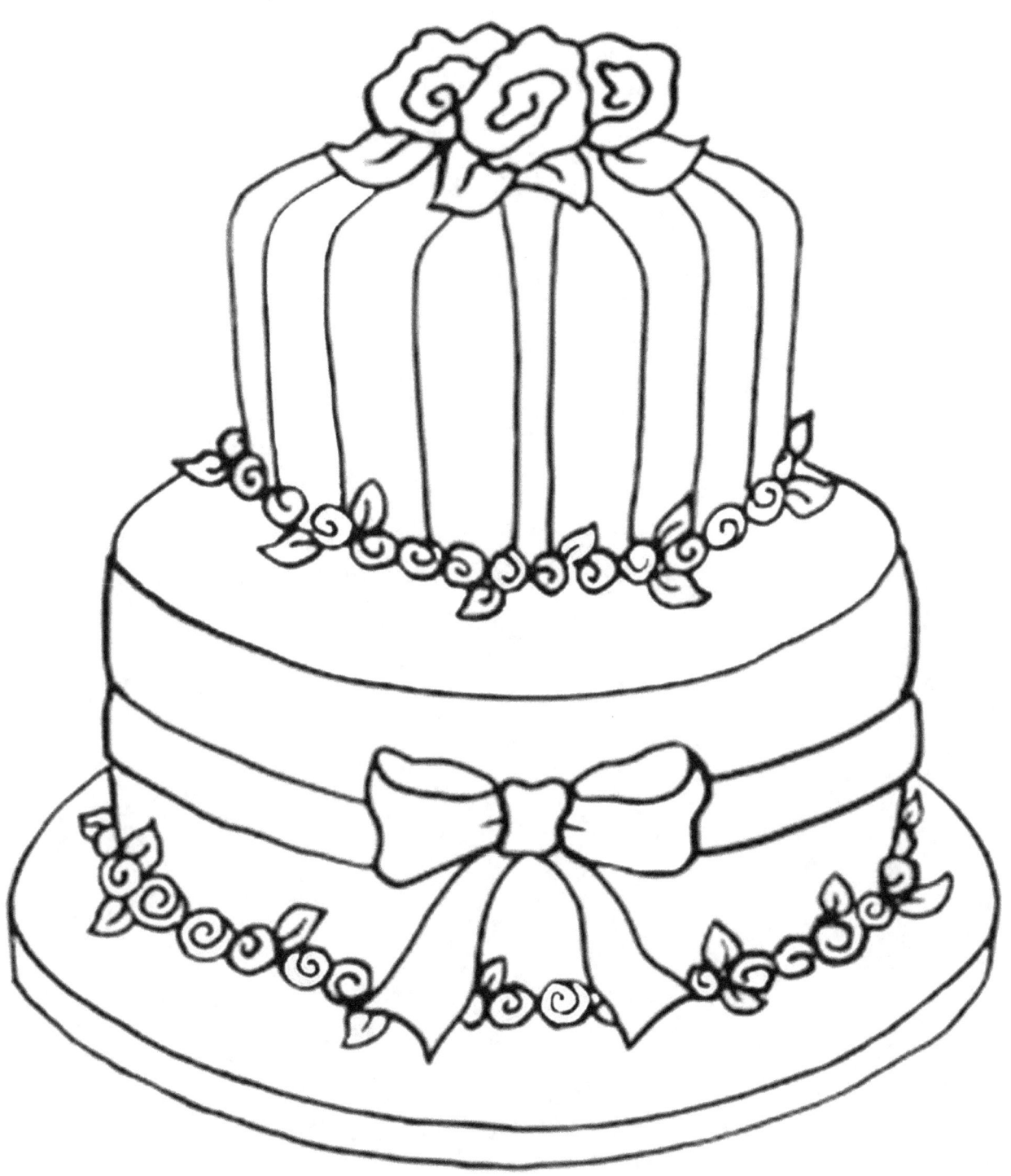

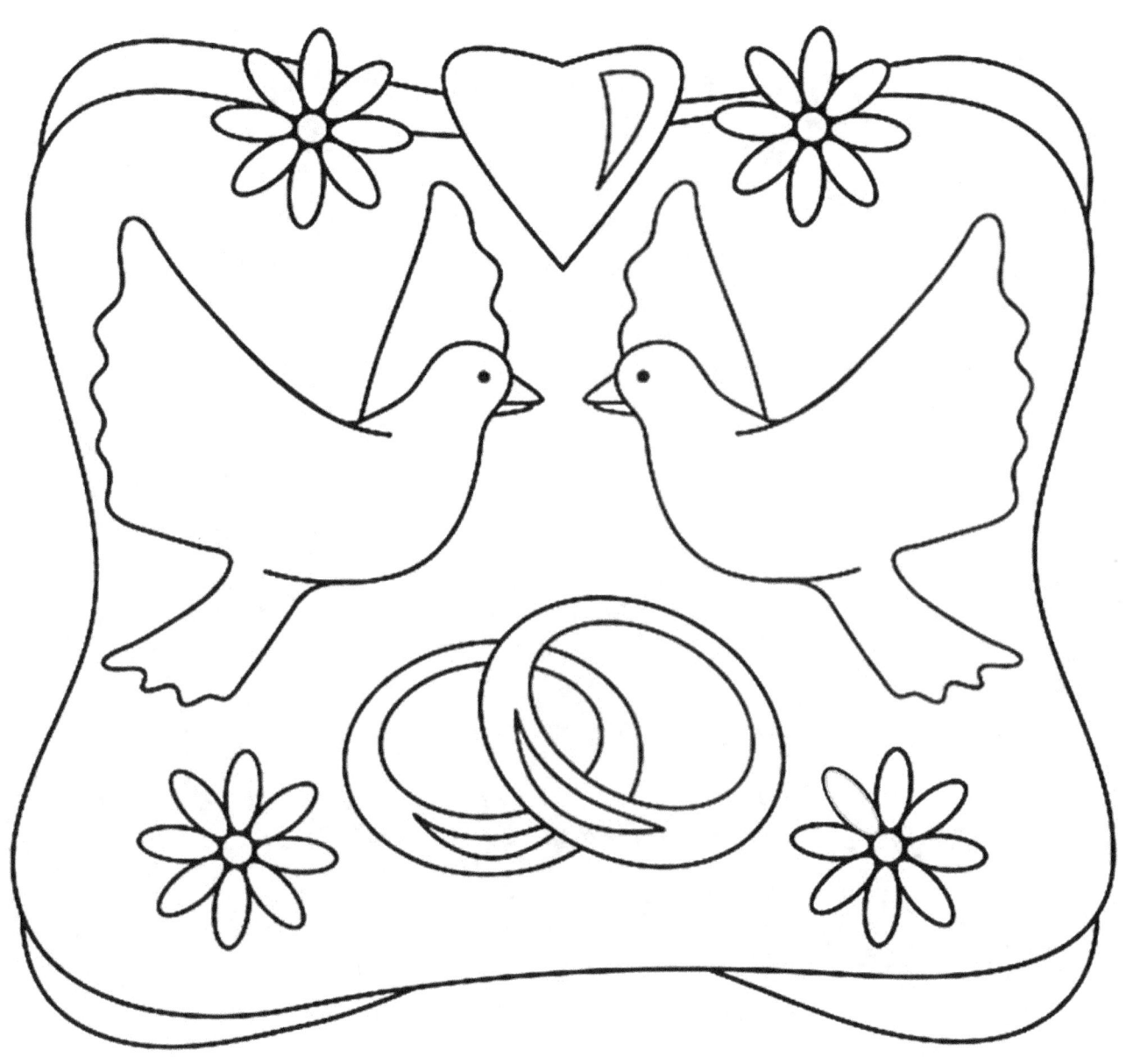

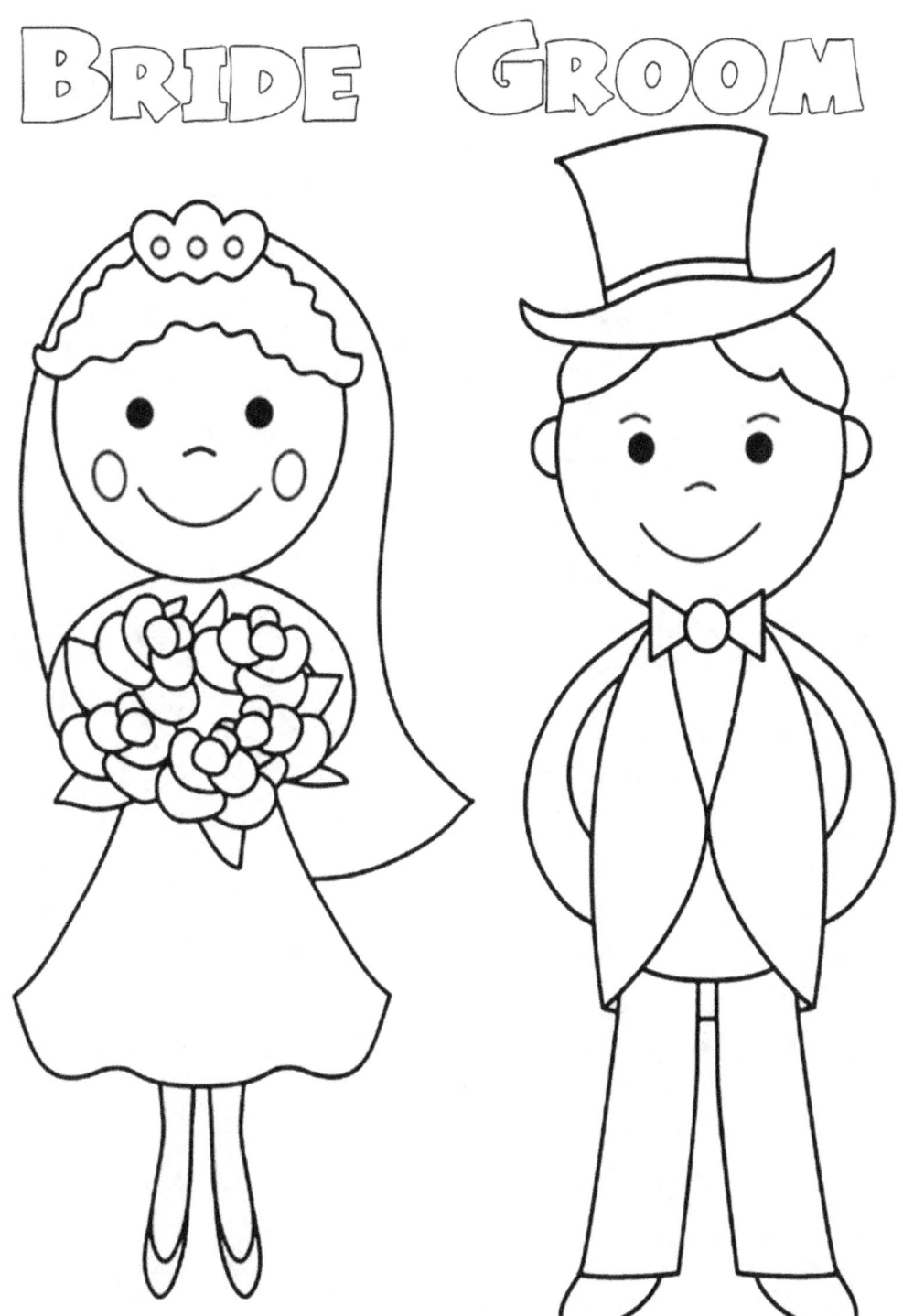

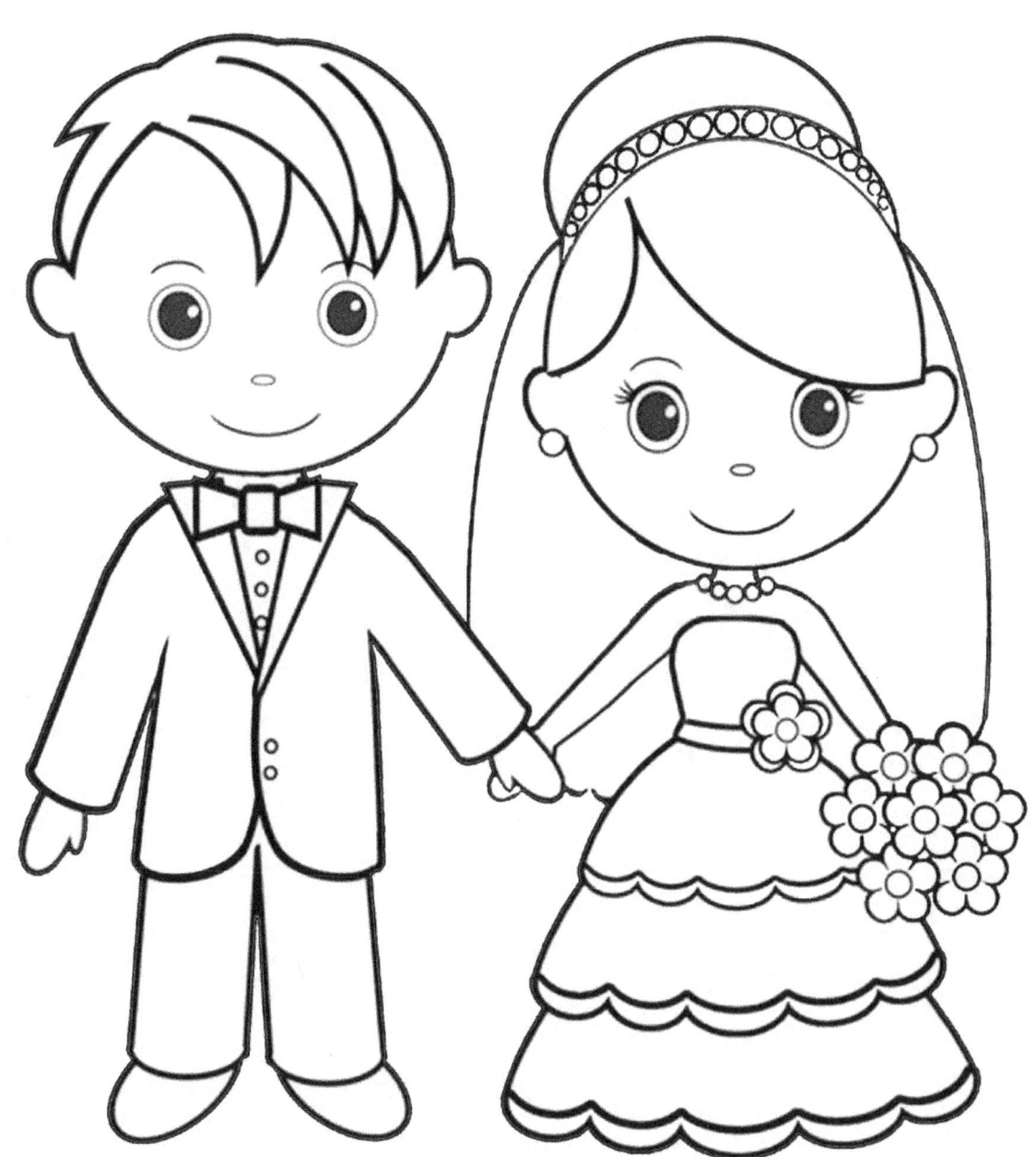

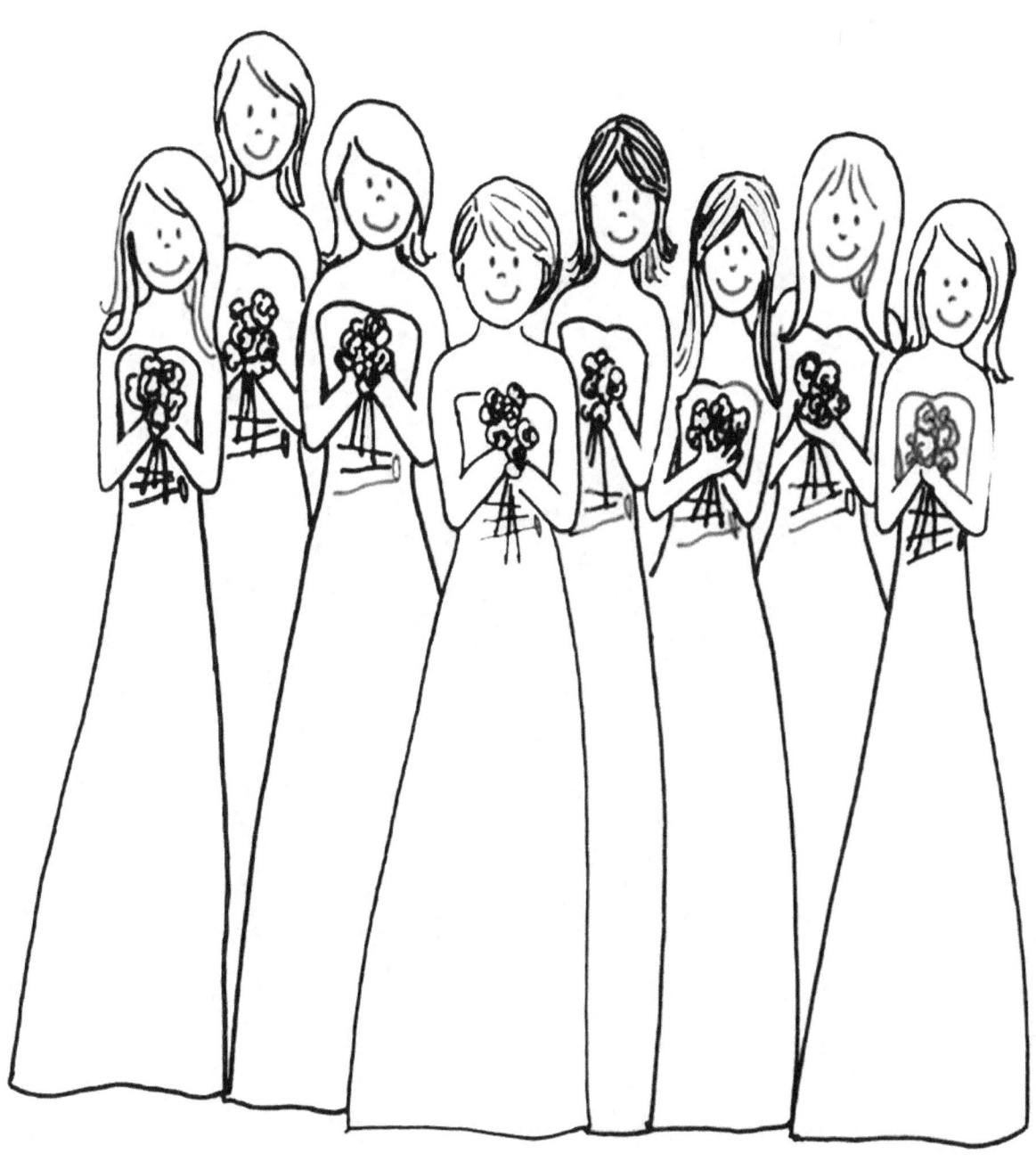

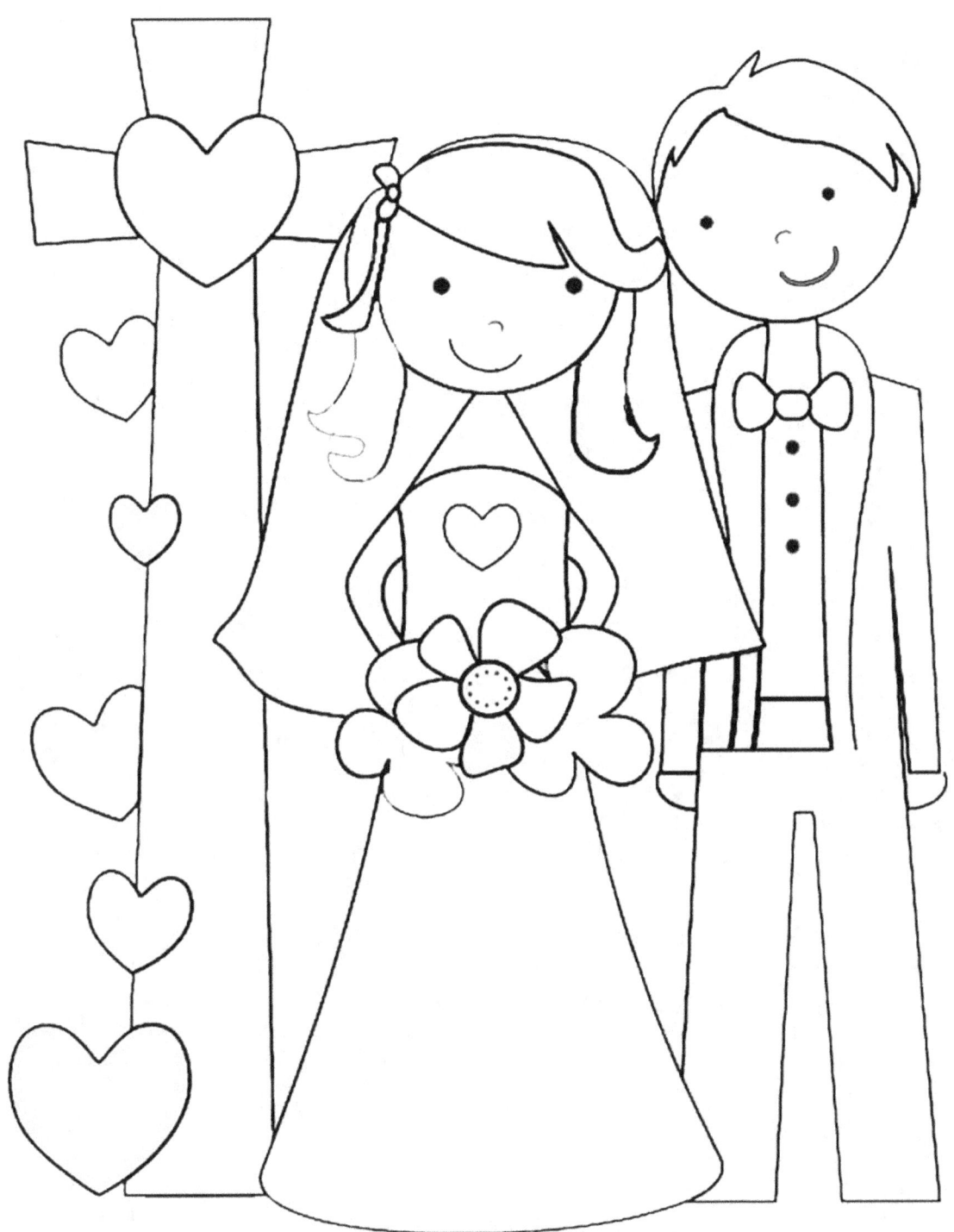

Rehearsal for Wedding

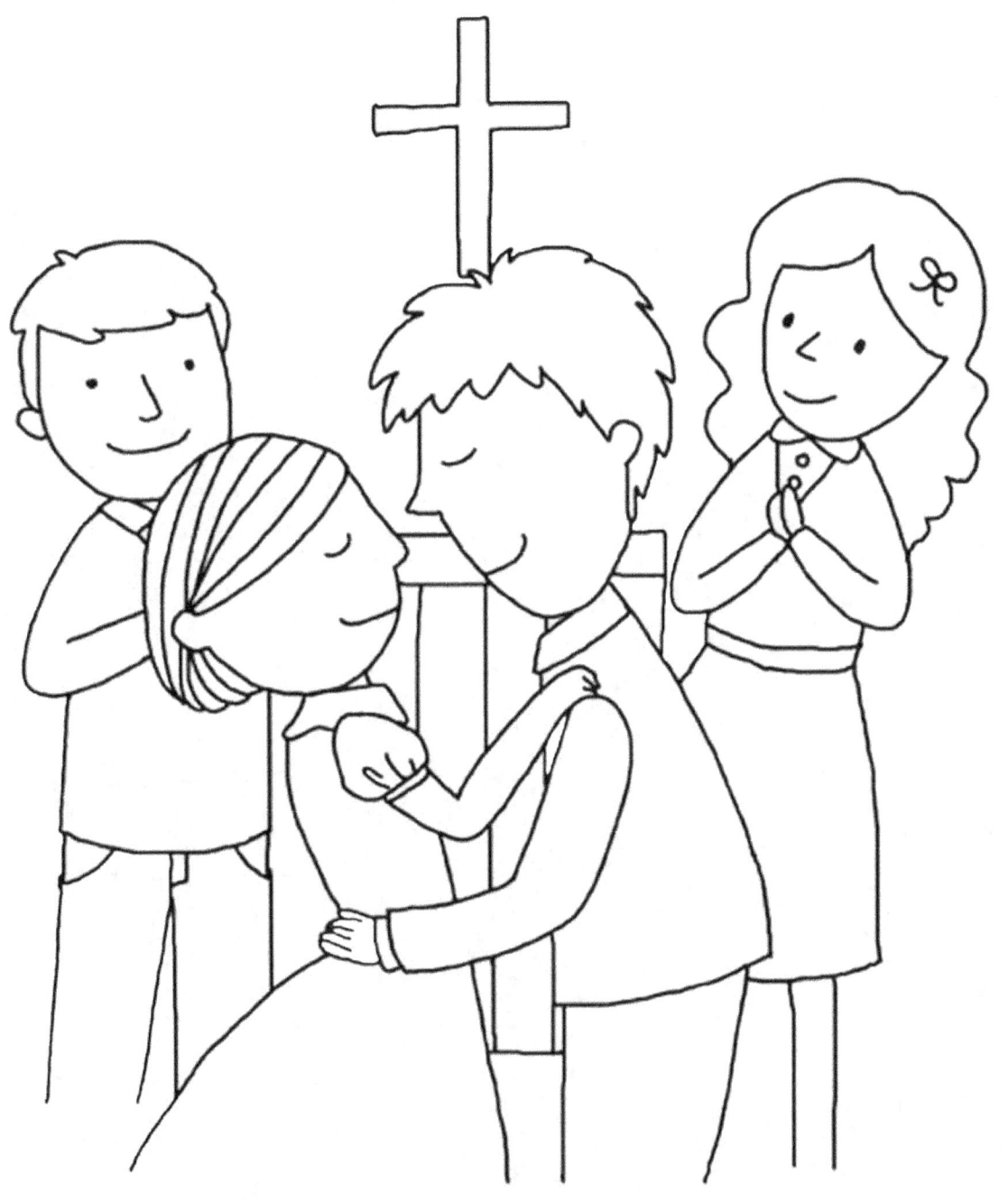

PUTNG ON THE RINGT

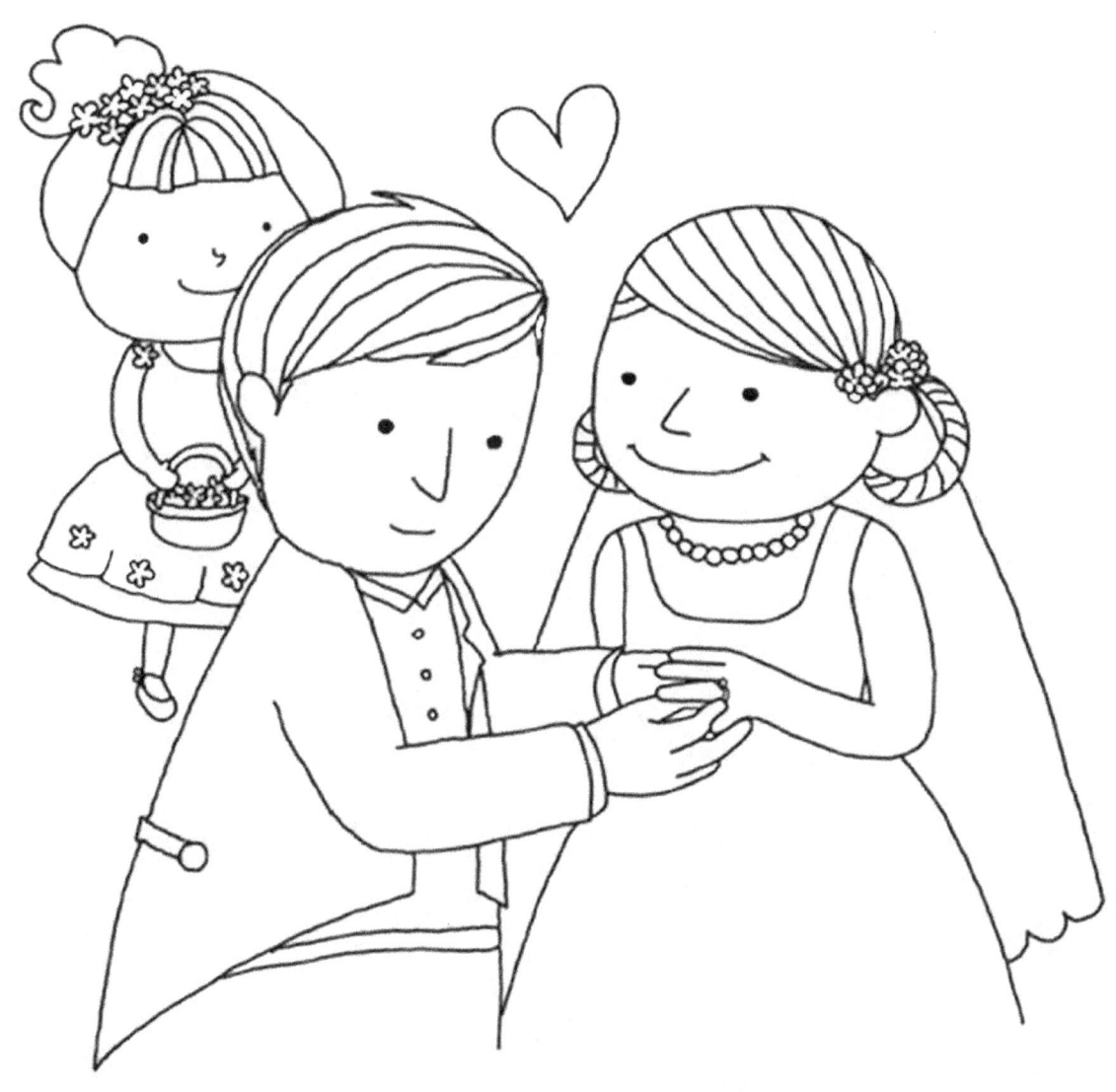

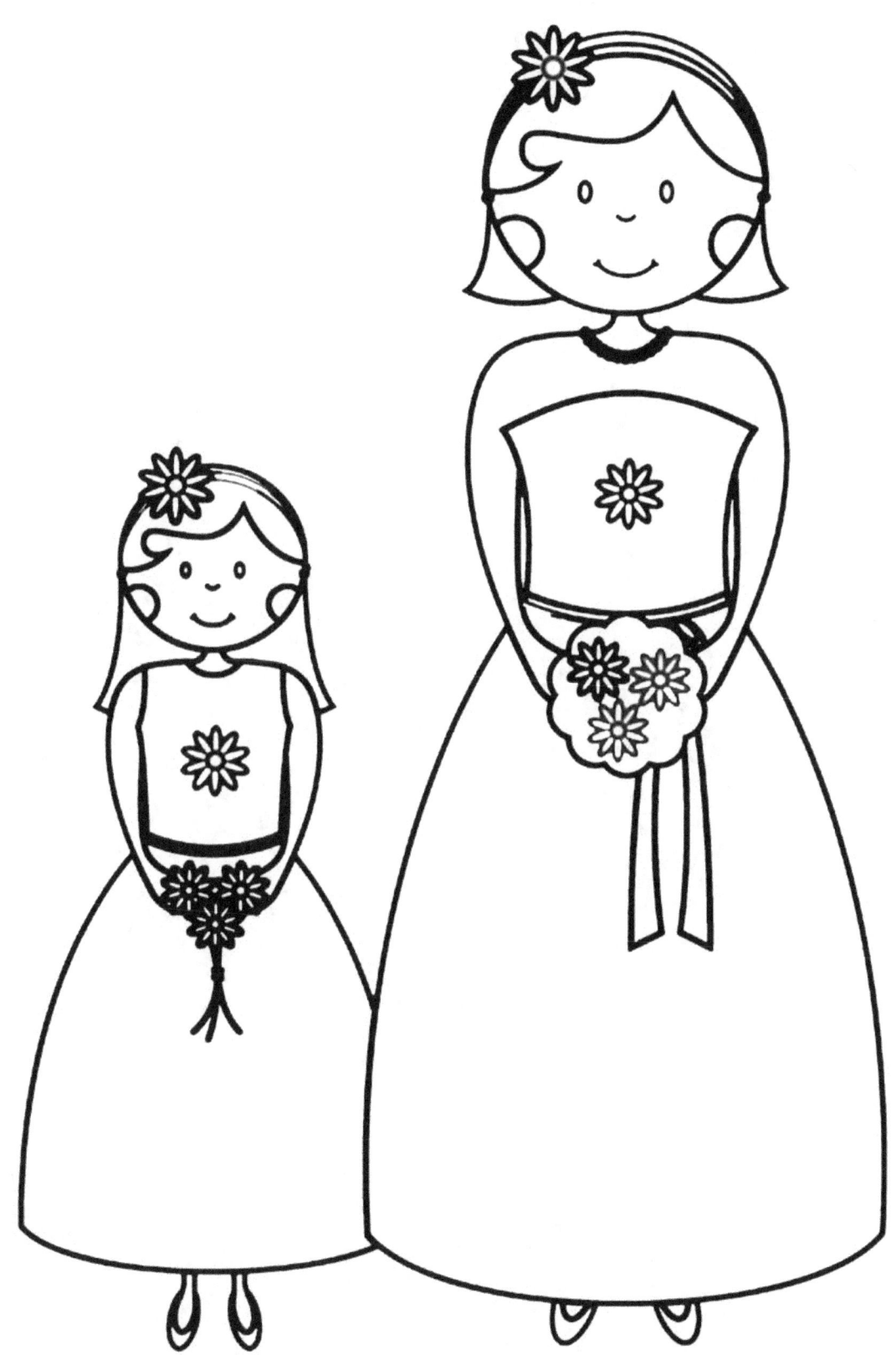

Flower Girl

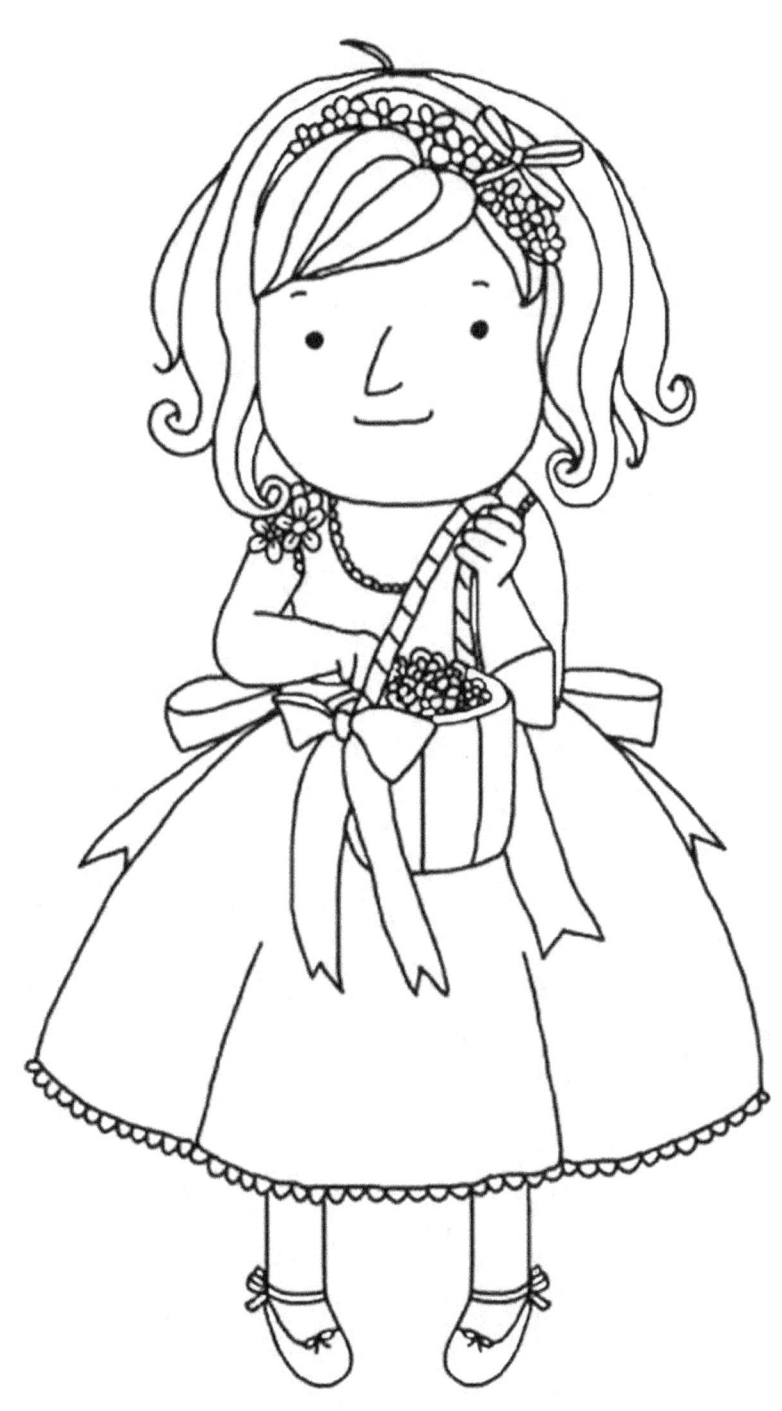

The Bride Throwing The Bouquet

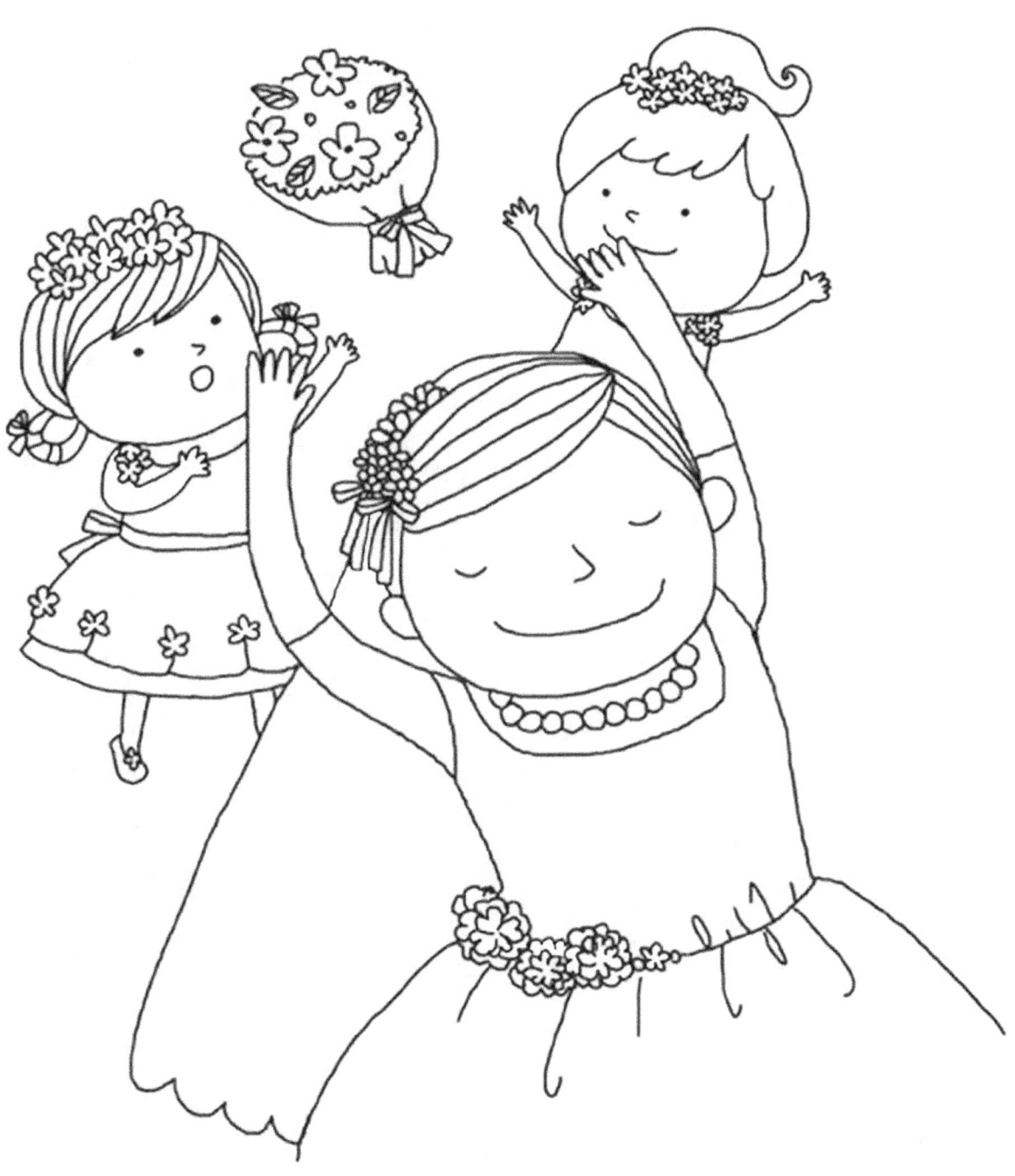

Wedding Reception

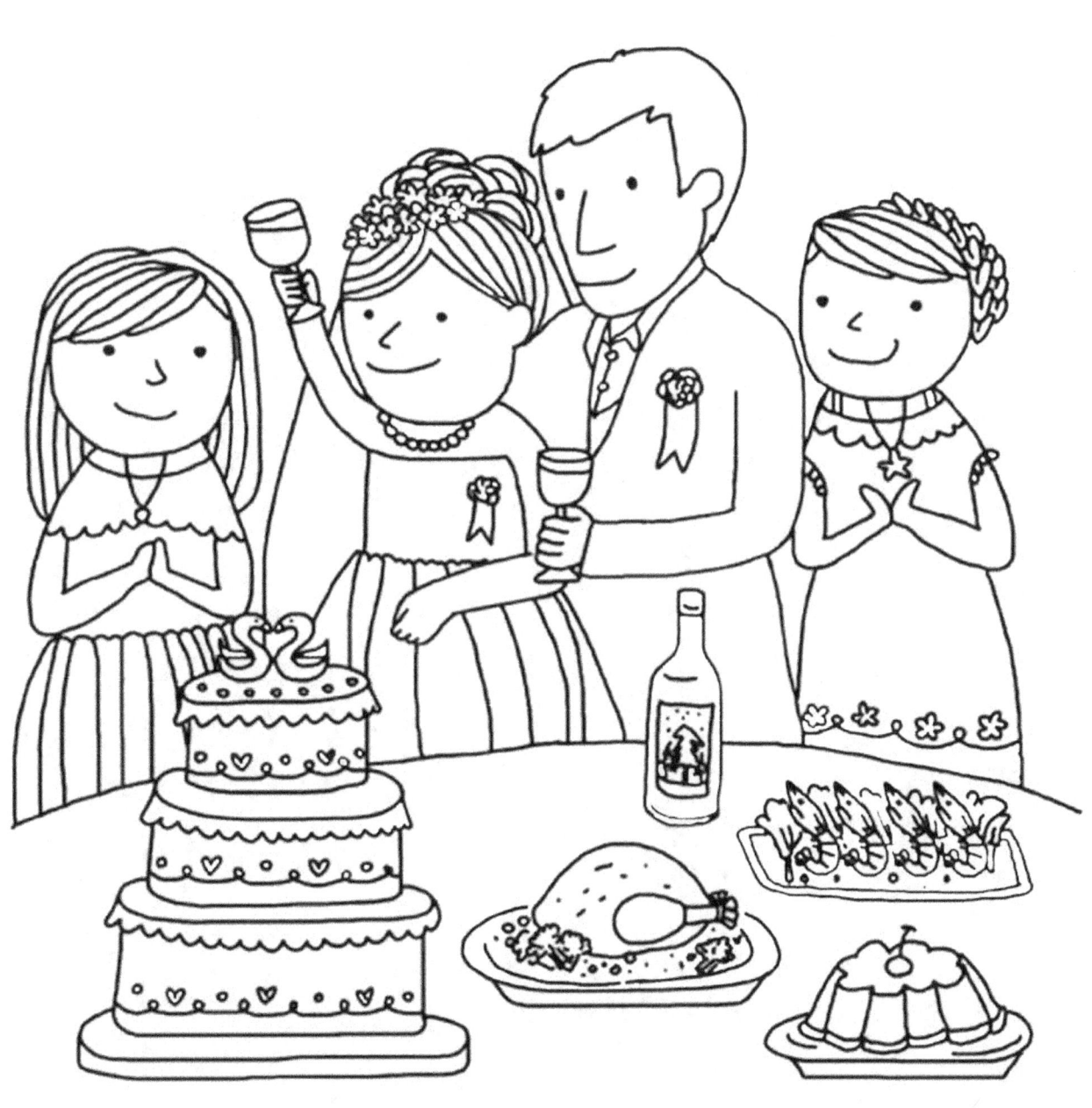

Wedding Dance

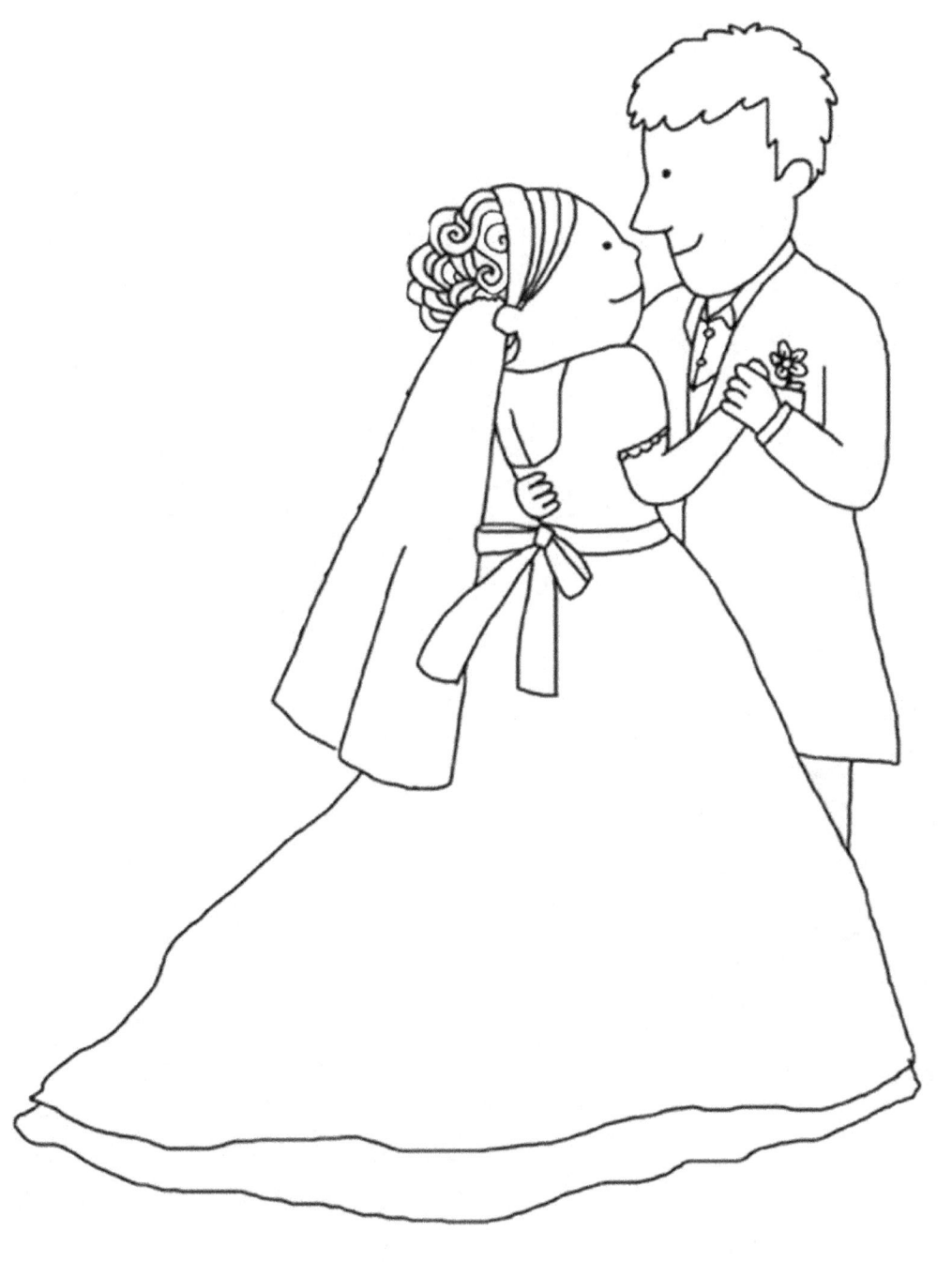

Taking off the garter

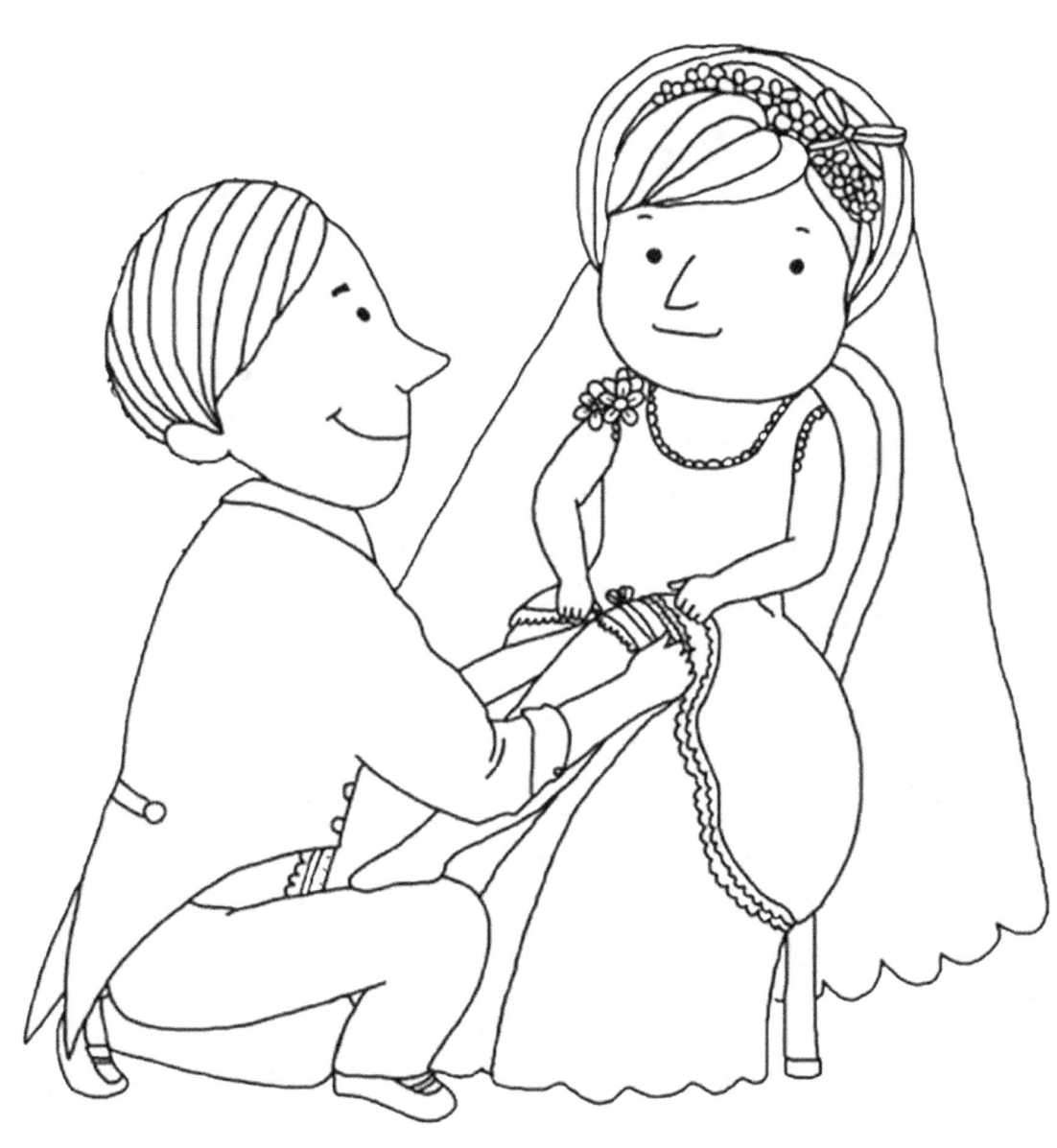

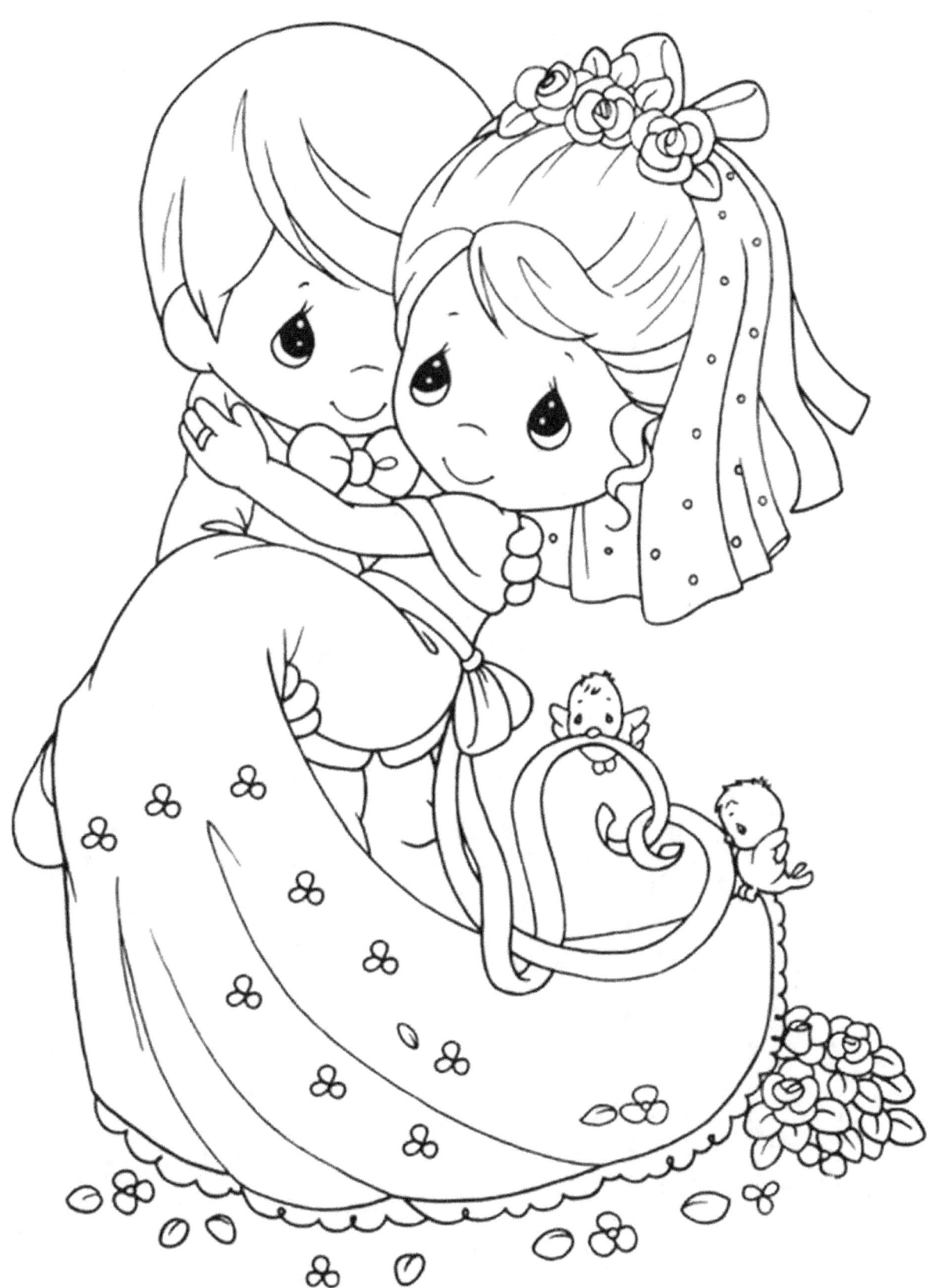

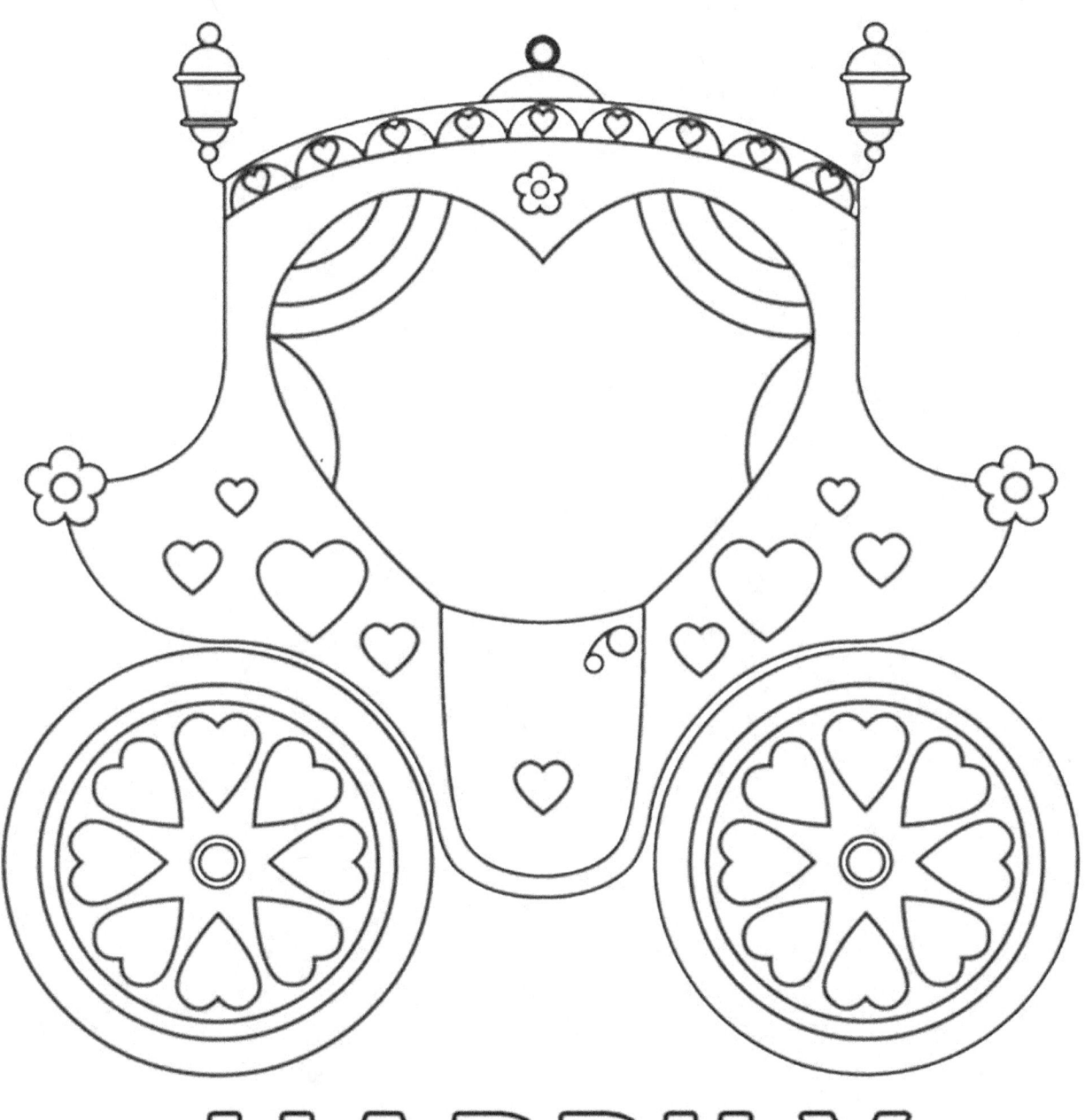